Lauri Robertson's poems are morsels to savor. She shares Proustian madeleines—hers, in a small crystal wine glass, just big enough for "a splash", that takes her back to her father. You walk with her through her garden of *fleurs sauvages*, run your fingers over the stone crevices of the French medieval village walls, eavesdrop on her conversations, with her mother, maybe with you, with all of us, lucky enough to listen. These poems, and especially those on memory, are nothing short of the most profound philosophical meditations on living, loving, losing, and growing old.

    Nancy Sherman

Listen. Put your ear to the door and you will overhear whispers, laughter, prayers and protests, wry observations and revelations from a mind trained to listen and follow the twisting paths of words. Lauri Robertson's poems in these companion volumes—*In Concert* and *Where Do the Memories Go?*—inscribe worlds. We turn the pages, encounter story after story. Every poem an image, a plot, mysterious and tangible. Loss, love, rage, solitude, self and memory, sentiment, the salve of creativity—our human lexicon—tendered by a feeling mind by turns wry, humorous, provoking, inflected with wisdom and curiosity—always honest. Nothing seems to come between Robertson and the page; she trusts it utterly and is wholly herself. Hers is a voice we want to hear.

    Anne Troutman

In Concert **is a convocation** of musings, both poignant and intelligent, laced with wry humor. We trace them along Ariadne's threads of memory. The poems, conceived and received as 'experiential', are light of foot—serious and not, skeptical of literary pretension. One might say that Robertson, as a psychoanalyst, is free associating, but these ruminations are deftly crafted. In the end, you will find in them a wise friend and, in her, an exceptional poet.

    David Barham

In Concert

Lauri Robertson

SPUYTEN DUYVIL
NEW YORK CITY

© 2021 Lauri Robertson

ISBN 978-1-952419-73-7

Cover photo by the author: "Chenonceau #2 2020"

Library of Congress Cataloging-in-Publication Data

Names: Robertson, Lauri Rosemary, author.
Title: In concert / Lauri Robertson.
Description: New York City : Spuyten Duyvil, [2021] |
Identifiers: LCCN 2021020293 | ISBN 9781952419737 (paperback)
Subjects: LCGFT: Poetry.
Classification: LCC PS3618.O316978 I5 2021 | DDC 811/.6--dc23
LC record available at https://lccn.loc.gov/2021020293

for Elise

"A **concert** is a live music performance in front of an audience."
"A **concerted reaction** is a chemical reaction in which…all bonds are formed and broken *in concert*."

Wikipedia

CONTENTS

I

I Want to Sit   3

Not Speaking French   5

Life is Not About Paris   7

Why I Live in the French Countryside   8

Insomnia   9

I Am an Atheist   12

I Want to See   14

Kicked Out by a Cloud   16

Home   17

II— IN CONCERT

Mozart   21

Schubert   24

Bach   28

Beethoven   33

Vivaldi   38

III

How I Became a Cat Person   43

Cat Quartet   46

Bird News   49

Crazy Love   54

All Your Names   56

The Fields Go   58

IV

for Merwin   63

You Think   64

Perhaps One Writes   66

Poetry   67

A Certain Kind of Poetry   68

Blurb   69

Process   70

So, I will Die   71

V

The Art of Being Satisfied with What You Have   75

The American Dream   78

Reading Obituaries   80

Song   81

Marriage   82

Coffee Shop   83

Din   84

I

I WANT TO SIT

I want to sit and watch the world
move into and out of focus
slivered, frayed—

my own life quiet now
if not ecstatic.
Marriage is quiet, quietly ecstatic.
Lucky, our old bones, fragile.
And, I'm almost an old cat lady
who I doubt could have dealt
with a child joyfully.

Decades of diligence paid.
It wasn't virtue, I was just too scared
to do anything else. I did
things that were hard
because everything was hard.

A little news, or more than a little
breaks the heart, everyday. I am
in France, far away.

But, in this little village
the monument stands—
half the young men dead back when
more than one or two
from the same families.

Was remembrance for a lost generation
honor or despair? And now
what is it?

Borders and horrors—
what we haven't invented
was invented for us.

NOT SPEAKING FRENCH

I didn't want to speak.
I wanted to wander in my own silence
which wasn't silent at all.

It made no sense, of course
because I needed many things—
to ask, fathom, opine— I needed

to be able.

Not only because it was hard
I didn't *want* to learn
or hear beyond babble

understand at all.
I wanted to be lost
in the sanctuary of no language

neither lonely nor abstracted
exactly, more like unruffled
freed just to *see* the world

or make it up.

Of course there was
embarrassment and shame.
I criticized myself. I thought

of pity or contempt for immigrants
grandmothers who came eons before
and never learned.

5

Now I was one. It was stifling
but I *wanted* to be a foreigner
(although I had no choice).

I came precisely to be
a stranger walking in a dream
with little distraction

or direction, conscious
of slow, deliberate minutes
counting themselves

or utterly adrift.

It was hard to explain.
Convenient as it might have been
to know, be known, belong
I had no desire.
Desire is all.
Oui?

LIFE IS NOT ABOUT PARIS

Life is not about Paris.
Life is about smallness.
One café or two
not miles of them

with throngs, flamboyant
or shy, searching
for what? Each other's
'energy'.

Life is about the pillow case
softened to threadbare
small arrangements
of small dried things, a room

in which to eat a boiled egg
like uncle Sydney
from the same egg cup
everyday.

Imagining that room
searching for it. Finding it
imagined. Light, yes
until the sun

etches the continuous
motion of shadows
and goes away
even in Paris.

WHY I LIVE IN THE FRENCH COUNTRYSIDE

There are children, and there is stone
beautiful ring-necked doves
which can be discerned in pairs.

The young children walk in pairs
holding hands on their way to lunch
more civilized than we ever could be.

They say *Bonjour,* and the damn doves
never stop saying.

What makes stone something to love?
Old and burnished, crumbling
or sculpted, graced with beams

and ironwork, the air
or patient, articulate solitude.

INSOMNIA

I have a penchant for taut sheets
bottom and top
rather perfectly arranged
a shallow pillow and buoyant quilt
not too much drag
at the ankles.

At my left hand there's a cat
usually facing backwards
but always within reach.

I think of those lovely tomb effigies
of noble women and their pets
emblem of *Le Moyen Age.*

Sometimes, I pretend
I'm alabaster, dead for centuries
and see how long I can go
without more than breath.

(After all, doesn't my desperate husband say
*No one in the history of the universe
has ever fallen asleep while talking and wiggling.*)

I lie and wait
for a thought that is not trivial
for expansion or animation
even an hallucination, something
to reveal something.

Someone called it *porpoising:*
diving and floating
in and out
of almost sleep
slow delirious
drift unveiling
almost
chandeliers.

What sacred engagement
for a sister to stone.

I wait and wait
and search for night
maybe stroke the cat
one more time

imagine *having* to get up
tyrannized by an alarm.
How blissful it would be
to lie still as memory.

Eyes continue to quiver
from light within their lids.

Yes, I like the bed sheets taut
as a trampoline
and tucked under my chin
just right.

The cat is now all akimbo
symmetry be damned
my hand cupping his little face
like a bandit's mask.

(How can a 9 pound cat
inhabit an entire bed?)

Where to go with this luxuriant
torture, the mattress warm
and smooth and happy

teasing each molecule
to sleep: perchance to dream
until none fights gravity.

Teasing incoherent syllables
light itself, out of existence
I rest in my sarcophagus sheets
from *luxury* to ancient *Luxor*
uxor beside a man who sleeps.

It's about a kind of perfection
that day will never bring
wrapped sweetly as a candy bar

remembering *hospitality, hospital, hospice*
have the same source.

I Am an Atheist

I am an atheist.
Years ago I might have said
I was an agnostic, but I
was just being polite.

I'm a dyed-in-the-wool
logical positivist, rational
observer, scientist, atheist.
(Also, an hysteric, if you
ask the right people.)

I don't believe in God.
But, that doesn't mean
I don't love. I have loved
with wild abandon, mercilessly
to the timber of my being
and beyond.

My father was an atheist. He taught me
God is in your heart, and in your head.

My husband is an atheist, too.
One day, some years ago
he spoke to the Unitarians on
"Why I am an Atheist".
He said something about
human, mortal, moral, this earth, now
and tears filled his eyes. Why?

I don't really know, and neither
did he, except that being an atheist
doesn't mean you don't cry.
I have cried enough to wash
the windows and drown the fishes.

I've loved and cried
clearing the muck
from the eyes of a kitten
or a giant.

I have loved and cried
unto a metaphor for God.

I WANT TO SEE

I want to see
a few sprigs of mint
in that egg cup
on an old slab of marble.

The display means little
but I would not like
to be blind.

I'd lose my mind
if I were blind

and could not see
the quotidian, inconsequential
arrangements of life— an herb
(loving the way *h* acts as a vowel)
in a crucible meant for an egg.

A leaf— look closer— it's serrated
or not, fuzzy or shiny, red
in the fall. Look more closely.

I would not want
to be blind.

Call it *feng shui*.
More than pleasing
it's durable. You can wake
and sleep to it, call it
a life, fortunate
cherished.

Or, shoes
sitting next to each other
neither work person's
nor fashionable, not sentimental
just lovely in the last
light of day—

light that makes
a simple object
whatever it may be
bespoke.

Say no more, I just
want to see. There are
too many words.
No more
please.

KICKED OUT BY A CLOUD

It was sunny, then it wasn't
lyrical then imagistic
then neither (thankfully).
What was left was a hieroglyph
depicting silence
all the silences.

And the sun came again
quickly, or all too quickly
then turned, the turning
kept coming and going
or coming and coming
and I was resigned
or indifferent or
paralyzed.

I watch the days
follow one another home like cowbells
my friend Kevin wrote
in High School, a city kid's
improbable pastoral
(slightly plagiarized).

"HOME"

(Forgive me, it was
a Thanksgiving assignment
for someone's grandchildren.)

Where you don't have to think
about where you are
in body or ether
or think at all, *I just
am.*

Belong is too requiring.
More, to float without fetter
do the damn dishes over
and over like a mantra
with solely the march of time
to prove one's existence.

Where the dishtowels
are chosen, old linen
someone else finds ridiculous
old, with holes
positively holy.

II
In Concert

II

In Concert

In Concert—Mozart

I'm sitting in a church
on a very hard bench
narrow, with no back
listening to Mozart's Requiem—
a very large, very old church
in France, overflowing
with the choir's *noir*
the listeners' silence—
two and a quarter centuries later
and not a day.

What music
invents the brain, releases it
as if we're sentient to be nothing
but creatures of grief
and ecstasy?

What dream rests
on what precipice
of what dream?

                    *

Let me tell you what I know.
You will search for your life
and then it will be over.
The search is the only.

Don't be docile
or smug. Being *yourself*
is not always a good idea.
Try to modulate
with auxiliary ballast
and gravitas.

If you come from trauma
large or small (don't we all?)
then heal as best you're able.
Better yet, help others
heal.

Touch the velvet of crows
far across the field, sing
their suspended melancholy

as if nature was not unkind
as if human nature, in particular
was not unkind.

                    *

The yards of hair
of old women
are tied behind them, their heads
nodding but still upright.

I can no longer
subtract my years from theirs
and find many left.

The end of immortality is clear.

I'm no longer arrogant enough
to feel sorry for them
but have begun to fear
the labor of their hair.

*

Music of centuries
but millennia of stone
carved and carried
how?

Even an atheist can see
God must be
this ability.

A daughter is tending an agèd mother
a child is sitting on a lap
or an animal is.

Renascence, Recuerdo
palpable
in the last forgotten universe.

In Concert—Schubert

In case it happens
a moment of extreme love
of the moment
have an old fashioned
pencil.

In case thoughts
come and collide
press upon the body
like melody, or lyric.

I am sitting in a church
once again, a very old church
listening to the pianist rehearse
tonight's concert— Schubert.

He's wearing
a bright orange t-shirt
reminding me of a prisoner.
Why mention this irrelevant detail?
Why not filter
instead of reify?

We are alone, save
for an elderly parishioner
with her head down, perhaps
recently widowed.

Some phrases he plays
over and over
(though I hardly notice).
Sometimes he shakes his hand
rather vigorously, or stops
abruptly. He turns
his own pages.

The height of civilization
this mélange of music
and ancient stone.

The sound engineer has appeared
plus a boy with yellow sunglasses
and blue polka-dot hat
in the arms of a man
with another man.

The child is three at most. Now
his sunglasses are below his nose
watching the orange pianist's fury
until the music stops.

The details of life seem
ordinary beyond the planets.
I remind myself that *art*
is the art of exclusion
wheat from chaff
but refuse, and choose
entropy.

Ah, the sound engineer
is actually a piano tuner!
There are riffs, an animated discussion
in a language I don't, and will never
understand.

Now, they seem to be
dismantling the piano
in some orderly, pre-ordained
fashion. *Bong, bong!*
Single notes and chords
more discussion, *too much buzz.*

It's been very hot, but without
much humidity. Now, it's cooling
welcomely. Hard on a piano
though. I think it's a D
that's gone bad, or maybe a G.
Bong, bong! What do I know?

(Nothing about how to navigate
between frank and chatty.)

A third participant has entered—
the tuner's boss, or the janitor
I can't tell.

The elderly parishioner is still here.
She's raised her head
in curiosity, or annoyance.

She and I, loyal.
I don't need her cane
yet.

But, there was another page
written with the pencil
that had become dull.
It was about the boy
and it's missing! It was about him
looking 'foreign', and wondering
if he'd been adopted.

In Concert—Bach

Still air, Bach
sounding squeaky
and women fanning themselves.

Still air, immobile air
or *yet air?*
Still life, inanimate
or *yet life?*

The audience is largely gray
as classicists are
these days.

The harpsichord
is out of tune, perhaps
it's the humidity. Certainly
the humidity. What gravity
on the faces of the young players.

Cherished Bach
but we're much in need
of something to help us ascend
the atonal stillness
of this night.

Will it come soon?
In what form? Opening
a door and finding
cool air has descended?

A last line?

*

My friend Kevin
always used to ask
What's the last line?

Was he sapient
or just impatient?

How interested can a high school student be
in another high school student's poetry?

Easier to write
than read.

Did Kevin ascend or descend
after his last line?

*

In the back hall
is what looks like
a Spanish family
or perhaps Portuguese
in work clothes.
The children are sitting
still as glass.

They may be gardeners
this time of year. Many
serve the front hall.

(Nothing wrong with honest labor
except for the divisions of labor.)

I wonder
if the woman at the door
let them in with expensive tickets
(like my own). I wonder
if they could afford...

But, after all, it is a church
(if I've neglected to say).

What if they've come
not for the concert
but to pray?

And, now I'm feeling uplifted
not because God is nigh
but because this family
has joined us, and is welcome
or welcome nor not
is here to stay.

Still life, yet life.
Kevin, what's the last line?

                    *

Even bad Bach is transcendent.

It leads me to think
of Cordoba, the Mesquite
a century here, a century there
of Christianity and Islam.

What of iconography, geometry?
Crying angels and arabesque?

Centuries when the world was larger
and there were more animals
more water, and endless promise

to lift us from this still night.
Still night, *yet night.*
Where is the last line?
Will it come soon?

      *

Now, for the encore.
The violin is more in tune.
Maybe it's warmed up
or we've cooled down.

They're playing softly
Bach, never mournful
but serious
and a little sad

(maybe like angels crying).

      *

Now it's the second encore.
The cello comes closer
to weeping, slowly
solo
a kind of melodic
animal cry.

I weep for the whole room
of mostly elderly
and for Kevin.

The family
has moved on.

IN CONCERT—BEETHOVEN

How complicated Beethoven is
how many notes, as if
not separate things
when I am looking
for simplicity.

How dense
the matrix of lyricism
and story telling.
Howl howl howl... How
profound, wild animals
dancing and devouring

endlessly.
I can't get away without saying
something irrepressible
wants to rhyme:
Ache with me.

*

My father always
played The Ninth
too loud

on the old
portable Victrola—
more than a little tinny—

and pronounced
his name *Beeth*-oven.
I wailed against the chaos.

Now, half a century later
in an ancient church
I'm thrilled

by crashing waves, racing
breath, mesmerized
by the violence—

this deaf man
demanding the keys
be pounded on, sweetened

for seconds then announcing
a catastrophic event
about to occur.

                    *

How brilliant the pianist is
rising and rising, what intricate
articulation, as if a language
clandestine keeper of memory.

I was thinking
how much my father loved him
perhaps enunciating the 'th'
merely to be theatrical.

Then came Geri, an old woman
who'd had a stroke. Would she still
know me? Would she have language?
All of a sudden, I remember

I'm in France, and have no language
as if I'd had a stroke. I might
lean over and whisper to her
Geri.

How is a deaf man speaking so clearly
through another's hands
two centuries later? Synesthesia.
Then one more, a younger woman.

Why them?

On her death bed, I leaned over
and said my name. Her face relaxed
almost to a smile. The week before
she told me she'd taken out

the Christmas ornaments
and written down where each
was from. They, she said would be
the keepers of memory

the music of ancient stone
deaf composer and limber pianist
a woman whose brain exploded
the whispers

that children of a dead mother
would be able to hear.

*

35

Now the audience
is clapping madly, suddenly
in unison, old arthritic hands
(the pianist himself would not risk doing)

as thank you
and request for more
begging or demanding
joy.

He sits down, happily
as do we, and the nurture
continues, like an animal
extending its arms

a child's abandoned toy
the last touch
of mercy.
Don't leave me.

Now he's playing
a second encore, *Für Elise*
we all played as children
at least the beginning.

It's as beautiful and complex
as memory itself. I imagine
I could still do it
at least a few phrases.

I imagine I can still feel
where to begin, in the
imagination of my hands
without fingers or voice.

*

We ask for so little here
a quiet place, a graceful old
French face at a concert
eyes closed for Beethoven
moved and appreciative—

old, as are many, as we
almost are. Who else
is left in the countryside
to live within stone
and remembrance?

We ask for a place
where imagination has gravity
and strangers are basically kind
to those outwardly modest.
It's not false that I smile

and feed stray cats. After all
they speak the only language
I can understand. We ask
to be carried to old age
by degree, losing the blood

of the world, exchanging dirt
for soil with grape vines
losing them both, eventually
the capacity for sorrow
regret, and everything else

by gentle degree.

In Concert—Vivaldi

In your short life
press your hand to my face
and see that it leaves
no impression at all

or one deeply in the flesh
of memory, a musical imprint
of something ineffable, or
which may not even exist.

There are four seasons
say Vivaldi and others.
We feel the prancing, doubtless
of fawns, and the snow.

Where is there to go
but to return again?

(I've heard serious musicians
make merciless fun
of what the rest of us love:
De de de dedede!)

What is there but evanescence
so familiar only weather
distinguishes the notes?
So accurate the shadow
recognizes its form?

The slender cellist is wearing
a drop-dead diaphanous dress
looking like Scheherazade
without the veils, nearly naked
in the desert heat, her shoulders
a living anatomy lesson
the large instrument her comfort
her beast of burden
and her weapon.

How young she is.
They all are. How long
will their fingers be able to navigate
the meticulous wooden curves?
Nimble and fleet, fleeting—

the repetitive notes that evaporate
instantly, poised for eternity.

III

III

How I Became a Cat Person

It was insidious.
Like everyone else (except
those bitten at a young age
or chased by the police)
I loved dogs. Cats
were somehow ancillary.

I loved dog personality
though have since realized
there's only one: *Ha-ah ha-ah
ha-ah Ha!* (Not exactly, but
pretty much.)

Cats, for better and certainly
for worse, are as individual
as we are. One needs to age into
feline subtlety. They

are old souls. Having no time
to take care of a dog helps.
Cats are ez-pz, except
they're wretched travelers

(known to poop in the carrier
after minutes in the car).

As a child I had one of each.
Cleo, the spaniel mutt
was the center of attention
in her quiet way
guardian and normalcy.

43

There's a photo of me
holding them both with little arms
indulging in their loving patience.
How do we know what we know
of childhood? Or, love?

That cat is tellingly unnamed
unremembered, as are others
through dog years and light-years.
Someone else's, they were just
there, unobjectionably there.

Those in recent decades, however
deserve *lengthy* chapters of their own
(I'll spare but skeletons, for now...):

Muskrat ('Scrat), a philosopher cat.
Marmalade the welfare queen.
Bradley-Snooks, frat boy, the only cat
with a sense of the absurd.

Camper-Moo, a cross between
a Mafia Boss and a Buddha.
Thee-Thee, the fat ballerina.

I didn't know for many years
they really do choose you.

The last beloved dog died
of old age, but not without
having been tortured by a few—
mischief and unrequited love.

Maddie-dog was devoted
but they were smarter.

Now, there's Charlemagne who
how, I'm not sure I can explain
while remaining a royal beast
his own cat and all that
expresses gratitude.

I have to admit, surprised
if not horrified, I've turned
into a fucking cat person.

CAT QUARTET

The spitting howl outside reminds me
we're a warring species, too.

And, if I think it will all work out
eventually, how wrong I am.

They'll shred each other, or the big grey bully
will my foolish little *boudin noir.*

Where did they learn *that,* and where will it end?
To the death, to the vet at least. To remorse?

No, only mine. I freed him for the night
to be as true to himself as we are.

       *

My stray cat, like a stray husband—
Get over yourself, you have to share him
with the old woman in the corner house

who thinks he's hers. *He's
a cat! Et, il est libre.*
He is free.

A stray adopts, is adopted by
a neighborhood, *a village,* and all that.
Get over yourself, he's not your fucking cat!

Though you love him more than life itself.
Do not trivialize anyone's love, whether
for children, or planetary occurrences

foreign as someone else's history
or one's own, forgotten, never known.
Why do I have to share my new

morsel of family, creature of the street
divine design, animal silence?
Speak!

*

They say a cat is a replacement for a child.
I say my relationship is nothing like that.

I feed him, yes, but grab and squeeze
such that if he were a child, I'd be arrested.

I *cheppa* him. (I believe this is a fake
'Yiddish' word my parents made up

meaning *to torture with affection.*)
I'm always there to be *intrusive, impinge*

and *fuse,* such nice psychoanalytic terms.
He, in turn, requires no college tuition.

But, there's much I don't like
and never would have taught.

Must everything be 'learned'
from mother's milk, the cosmic

sequence of kitty genome?
I, human, am actually nice to mice

and, praise be, love birds. Bunnies, too
(although, in France, join in eating them.)

                    *

Night cat—
to see him leap

in the streetlamp-lit light
chasing bugs, or invisible bugs.

Even the swifts quit after dusk
exchanging for bats.

Fabulous pirouettes!
Gravity means nothing to a cat.

Gravity means nothing if
the people rise, if atheists ascend

to heaven. A mote of no-see-ums
begs him to Saint Vitus dance.

Why can't I fly, or at least
quarrel with the earth honestly?

BIRD NEWS
for Vernon Laux (1955-2016)

Now it's happened. Why didn't I pay attention
two days ago, to the cat, terribly curious
about something around the damper?

I thought, perhaps, it was a bug
I couldn't see.

Then, yesterday, a different fireplace
but sharing the stack, great fluttering
left no doubt— a dove.

I was able to free her
and she flew out the window
minus a handful of tail feathers.

This led to a need for the shop vac
for soot and crumbs accrued since the last
chilly evening, a few walnut shells.

But, waking this morning, slowly
barely conscious, I thought to check
the other fireplace, the cat's inquiry.

A rain of crumbs once more and, oh
two dead baby birds with pre-feather fluff
the size of small mice, fellow prey.

Tears in my eyes. Why hadn't I listened?
I should have known, or did, and just
didn't listen. For a moment I imagined

49

I could have saved them, held them
in my palm, safe from the cat, fed them
and watched them grow, fledge.

Then, *no*, they were too small
and, it's a very tall chimney.

I gender the dove as female
because the symbol of what we used to
call *peace* always seemed to be.

And because, in that drift to sentience
did I know what I'd find in the other flue?
dream their mother had gone looking?

I hope there are others, three, four, five
still in the sky. I hope the tailless Columbid
will survive. My husband says

she won't be able to balance.
Perhaps she is a mourning dove.

                    *

Bird News was the title of
a weekly radio program about birds.
The star was charmingly enthusiastic.

His motto, and closing words, were always
"Keep your eyes to the sky."

Life being local, we got to know him
enough to accost him in a restaurant, and say
"I love your show, and I don't even like birds."

My husband went bird-watching with him once
and said he practically jumped up and down
like a little boy when they saw a bird.

He, the birdman, died too
a few years later, a few years ago.
Please tell me you remember him.

Why do we have death? Silly me, there's always
been death, all kinds of death, guaranteed.

I have to remind myself that birds
perhaps in particular, meet all kinds of fates.
Perhaps that's why there are a lot them.

After all, doesn't a seeming infinity of doves
drive us crazy with incessant cooing?

Perhaps it was just a sad day in Birdville
that nothing can undo. (Would that sad days
could be undone.)

I do worry if they're safe
around the cat, though they mostly are.
He's mostly a chatty voyeur.

And, doesn't nature have its ways
her ways, of denying that nature
in any imaginable way, is safe?

Keep your eyes to the sky.

*

The next time it was not a surprise
when the thing fell down the chimney.
I knew immediately because the cat
knew immediately. Yes, a bird
with feathers and all, a fledgling
speckled, with a tiny curved beak, a hawk
though later I thought, maybe an owl.

Take him/her/it/they inside
or leave out, (leave out the pronoun)?
The latter, I thought, so a parent might find
unlike last time, when understanding came
far too late. Problem was, we were

in the middle of a 100° Fahrenheit
canicule, crazy dog star heat wave.

I will not go out to look for a carcass
or see if the water I left had been drunk.
I'll imagine instead the creature found it's own
prey or life-affirming shade, or love
and flew as if destiny.

Unlikely, I know and, surprisingly
again my tears flow. Is sorrow

always the sorrow of nature? The aberrant
nature of us, with our wars and chimneys?
One last migration into the pyre?

This is not allegory, or a last moment to soar
like some other, successful fledgling, just
a small horror that absorbs me

perhaps absurdly, the belated amendment
of ignorance. It was not a surprise
but why am I, as if eviscerated
surprised?

CRAZY LOVE

for Teju Cole

Crazy love of crazy detail—

I have to photograph
the antique watering can
brass at the spout.

And terracotta roof tiles
of the house next door
ankle height on our *petit balcon*.

The cat tried to climb them.
I told him, "No!"
Did he listen? No.

Then, one fell or, rather, slid
with a clatter. Apparently, they're
held by very little. The cat fled.

I never tire of looking at clay
upon clay, orange to crimson
color evincing color.

What could be less interesting?
But, the more you look
the more you see, trust me.

Now, I have to reach
for the camera again.
An ancient wooden beam

has joined the conversation.
Didn't Freud say something like
The past joins the conversation?

ALL YOUR NAMES

When you die
they use all your names
Yiddish, baptismal, nick
family, middle, maiden
disowned given and sur-
etc.

I will have *Rosemary*
in the middle for grandma Rose
whom I never met. But, *Mary?*
Who names even a 3rd generation
Ellis Island, ethnic only
American Jew, "Mary"?

(Then there was my husband's
evil stepmother, *Rosemary.*)

Ah but, ...*rosemary, that's for remembrance.*

And, how should our names sound
remembering us, or not, to assume
or not, black or white, Arab or Jew
Indian, Chinese, get my riff-drift
German, French (we wish)
ending with consonant or vowel.
What status to whom?

Whom else would you want to be
in this world, rich or poor
without arrogance or shame?
Which is more desirable
or offends?
All my names! Are names all?

Weirdly, I've spent a while
thinking of names (and nicknames)
for my feral black cat
a consoling kind of list.
(Lists are consoling for some).

And, he went from "Blackie"
(as the French neighbors called him)
Sauvage Othello Panthère
to Charlie, short for Charlemagne
(say it *Sh...*) which rescued the situation.

*What's in a name? ...a Rose-*mary
by any other... Merely descriptive?
Proprietary, memorial, affectionate?

I love you Charlie, Sharlie
Bunny-Skins, Bun-Bun, Squirrel-Face
Feathers, Puppy-Fish

signed

Lauri, Lorki, Laurqui, Rosemary
Laurihare
Lahare
L'hare
Hare

...where the mountain hare has lain.

THE FIELDS GO

The fields go fallow
the vines go yellow.
Not much happens here
(unless rhyme is an event.)

The feral kitten is tame
almost a cat.
(I love that the French word
is *sauvage*.)

Birds flee him now
he's graduated from bugs.
I don't like that part at all
(nor his penchant for bats).

The seasons change
but not much else.
You have to pay attention
to notice anything.

You have to listen
to the endless sky
the monotonous clock
you can't stop.

Of course
there are different birds
with different seasons.
It will be years or forever

before I know them all.
The fields are groomed
as Godiva's tresses.
The tarragon is dry.

Not much happens at all
yet it's impossibly beautiful
and improbable contentment
envelops us.

IV

VI

FOR MERWIN

on what was to be his last birthday

You were my youth, a young Adonis
when there were still a few animals.

A few of your words were my credo
scholarly mystic speaking abnegation to despair.

Then decades later, enshrined in a university
for the night, a sweet face turned only sweeter.

Now I see only photographs
with a tear for the beautiful, lucent fragility.

Someone once said they heard you say
to a young person asking how to be a poet:

Listen.

How long it's taken me to silence the blare.
You were my credo. I wish I had listened.

I wish I'd been able to listen.

You Think

You think there has to be
something more, or more eloquence
then retreat from lyricism
beaten like a race horse, breathless.

You think *high* is no good
proletarian too 'pasture-all'
quotidian just plain boring.

I thought, bursting with emotion
I had something to say.
Emotion is for teenagers.

Silence, please.

Yet, those brick chimneys
absolutely still, crying for repointing
with terracotta pots like fezzes
are too noisy!

Let me try to explain
the tension between inner and out
the arc of a distant tree, swaying
even antennae marring the view
I've come to love.

The inner must swarm
with gratitude

for *du vent après la canicule*
(wind after the heat wave)
time to mean nothing
to anyone, not even oneself

for the rooftops themselves
so motley they could never
be memorized:

limestone and state
mortar, wood somethings
(I don't have a word)
broad and narrow
bleached and calcified
moss, dead and alive
a remnant of vines.

Even the cleverest student
(who must work hard, too)
couldn't learn by heart
a corner of the universe
so small it can't be named.

Commitment to memory
is only useful anyway
until the next deluge.

Perhaps One Writes

Perhaps one writes
to find a voice
as if it wasn't there—
that tree falling
in the abandoned forest.

Or, quite there but
so internal it can't be heard.

Or, one wishes thought could
simply be transcribed from
the brain's matrix of ticker tape

the 200 labyrinthine miles
of catacombs under Paris.

Which way does one go?
Does it matter?

Or, as if thought is a waterfall
in a rainforest
at an amusement park.

POETRY

It seems for sure
more people are writing it
than reading it

with great urgency
inside and out
entirely necessary
in times like these.

I asked my beloved mother-in-law
who lived through at least one
World War, what she thought of now.

She said, "I no longer believe
Well, at least it can't get any worse."

So what if we're ManuFActurING poets
at pace with investment bankers—
bleeding hearts and daydreamers
vs. scoundrels and thugs.

What kind of culture is this?
Democratization of dross.

I think of James Wright
"Depressed by a Book of Bad Poetry..."
Depressed by a book of bad poetry?
I'll give you something to be depressed about!

An urgency I'm glad neither she nor he
is alive to see.

A Certain Kind of Poetry

Why imagine you can
put more words in
than anyone else, that this
particular asphyxia is a mark
of excellence and certainty
if not formal proof
that you are loved.

As if articulated while exercising
too hard, or *making love* as it
used to be called, now in the vernacular
sex no one really has time for anyway
because they're running, going
impossible to know where— nowhere—
except to what used to be known
as *Hell*.

It comes on like a quick fever
a lingo cacophony disease
that sometimes stays.

And, please don't get me started
on the particularly vexing peculiar
cadence of *viva voce* enjambment!

BLURB

These poems are mutts.
You may or may not like them
as is inevitably the case.

They veer from the quotidian
to the extraordinary, each of which may
or may not be objectionable.

They're original in as much as
to paraphrase Tolstoy
everyone's whining is unique.

The poet licks a sword of humor
to slice pedestrian pathos.
How can music be banal?

They're chatty or callisthenic
a little like whiplash at the wheel
of a student driver, or when

trying to study a foreign language
you forget your own.
They're cranky and indulgent—

purse your lips.

World literature needs another poet
like this like the world needs another
fill in the blank.

PROCESS

To do something very common, in my own way.
—Adrienne Rich

I could revise it
until the cows come home
until the cows have come
and gone, until the fucking
cows are dead, or have
grown wings, become supreme

celestial beings, creatures
of nourishment and discontent
nourishing our discontent
with soft muzzles and damp breath
more intelligence than we grant
others we eat less.

Is it a fashion of the moment
or, possible to make something
most miniscule that will last
like a cow's horn made into
a caviar spoon or a button
a shofar?

So, I Will Die

So, I will die
on a pile of dead poetry
half written, half eaten
by wild animals or insects.

That will be all that's left
along with a corpse, fresh
or sour with slow departure
or missing entirely, vanished
like a cat who didn't come home
all urgency vanquished
the world in pain
deeper than our impotence
the children I didn't help escape.

Quotidian, anti-imagistic
anti-lyrical— what is enough?
Narrative, but whose story
can possibly be told and
it still be possible to know
the beauty of the world.

V

The Art of Being Satisfied With What You Have

First, have enough:
somewhere to live
neither too, too cold nor hot
if quirky, then worth it
for some charming feature
convenience, price, or view
plumbing that works (mostly)
food, and a modicum (or more)
of safety.

None of it has to be ethereal
or divine, blessed, otherworldly
or otherwise terrific. Then
say like a mantra:

I have enough.
I have enough.

Now it (life, that is)
is all a quest, or a gift
or the gift of giving up
questing.

Be sure to be
abundantly grateful.

*

Wealth:
If, perhaps, I envied it then
(surely I envied it then)
I loathe it now. I loathed it
then, too, but differently
now, without the envy. Now
with pure, visceral revulsion.

Not to worship asceticism
or, certainly, not poverty
not to eschew all *objects d'art*
but, I now believe with all my heart
modesty, moderation, reserve
are the last vestiges of worth.

The rest, give away, just
give it away, give to friends
those who are languishing
and animals. Skip enemies.

Give it as if the true meaning
of generosity was not sacrifice.
You sacrifice nothing
if you have enough.

*

Reparation:
There is nothing
that will conquer your sorrow.
No *thing*.
It is old, and it is forever.
It's an ancestor you didn't want
or even have, but who claimed you
like your bubbling up, your hair growing.
Would that it had been different
a different gift.

THE AMERICAN DREAM

My mother believed
in The American Dream.
I'm not even sure exactly
what it meant to her.

But, I've lived it. Post war
Velveeta, Spam, and all.

Her father was a turn-of-the-century Jew
conveyed from Ellis Island to Denver(!).

By one account, he had a horse
named Charlie, and a linen cart
and/or was a plumber.
They had a toilet in the window
of which she was ashamed.

But, I've lived it. Good luck
and hard work, sure— some of the former
made by the latter, some simply driven
by the anxiety of not wanting to be
left in the American dust, or worse.

Not wanting the trenchant stigma
of mental illness— hers, that child-like
mother of mine, whose grandiosity
sweetly dreamed...

So, like a script, written in hieroglyphics
from particular family fragments, I became
and became, and cherish that reality
in every way.

Now, wandering into retirement
(not even metaphorically a Jew in the desert)
sad for the particular nightmare
America has become
I think of the dream.

This morning in an hour and a half
without leaving the house, I made
6x what a cashier in Kansas
made all day.

I don't want to give it back
yet, but am hardly proud
The American Dream
is a dream.

READING OBITUARIES

I no longer like these lives
once read with regard
now contempt.

Good, it was long, eighty-something.
You're allowed to die of anything
you want. (I won't suspect suicide
or imagine it undue.)

And, maybe you were nice
philanthropic even, well-
meaning, but I hate

the right parents, right schools
corporations and garden clubs

the privilege
you were born into
a hopefully now dying
unitary ideal of civility.

I know it's not your fault
but don't brag about it
especially from the grave.

Say you were humble
and grateful. Say you loved animals
what you did for whom.
Repent.

SONG

Let's not be saccharine, let's not be snide.
Let's not be melancholy
or vulgar (unless warranted for emphasis).

Let's not be evil, degenerate, crass
hostile or brassy, senselessly aggressive.
Let's not leave these indictments unexamined.

Let's not be harsh, critical or drunk
(unless it's a perfectly fizzy day).

Let's not be envious (not too envious) or glib.
Let's neither nor all day.

MARRIAGE

I like my bread
salami, vegetables
whatever you can cut
cut on the bias.

It's more elegant
that way. And, there's
more surface area
to sear for flavor.

He cuts them
blunt, in chunks
no matter how many times
I've asked him not to

nicely— perhaps merely
preference, and why
should I be the one
to get my way?

Or, a kind
of perpetual warfare
willful, perpetuated
with blades.

COFFEE SHOP

Lost in their relatedness, or un...
To sit with strangers, in proximity, why?
In silence, or as tree roots converse
with their own kind, a family of others.

A particularly scruffy collection of old men today:
Retired? Homeless? Trustafarians? Poets?
Wait, several are not so old, fifty maybe, eccentric
or is it style? The pleasing oddity of wingtips.

And oh, one I saw at the library last week.
It closes at noon today. Coffee is the open option.
Does he wonder why *I'm* here? He looks
less fortunate, or fortunate by some irrational choice?

To sit and read lightly, with the house blend and a snack
facing that window with the sun streaming in
a musical rise and fall of chatter
punctuated by gentle laughter

unselfconscious, as I am not, looking up
now and then, to look into the blue beyond.

DIN

It started out
I had so much to say—
mountains and skies
slate roofs, tree tops
all the big tall things
or so I thought
until I got too old
perhaps to care

or heard the din of the world
throbbing with incessant *cris du coeur*
pain, idiocy, lack of integrity, even
lack of novelty.

I wanted to say beautiful things
but it seemed unkind, tone deaf
in light of unimaginable
darkness and thirst.
I wanted to say smart things
but they were really more
like smart-ass.

Thoughtful, intelligent, professional
things? Blah and blah, and blah, blah.
Devotion to *authenticity*— almost worse...

Sorrows of many, sorrows of few
unique sorrows without voice
in any language.

And, the sorrow of animals
for which I feel particularly responsible—
my species against yours
we've all but annihilated.

Where is there to go?
Righteous rage, and bourgeois fools.
No, not nihilistic, just heavy-hearted
however radiant the sun in my own room.

There's something about being in France
the land still soaked with boyish blood
of two wars to end all wars
plaques in villages with names remembered
in almost remembered history
our civilized West, our last breath.

We make war not love
and are proud of it.
The cacophony of the world
has drowned the words
and drowned the meaning
of the words.

                *

Can it really be *the world*
out there? I who was so
gentle, forgiving, tolerant
can't sleep, am screaming
but can't speak. Can this
really be? After a lifetime
of thinking pain can be
personal, psychological
existential?

Humans beings are unable
to govern themselves.

Let me say, sometimes
I'm glad I'm old, and dear
migrants, oppressed, shredded
abandoned, just breed the shit
out of these assholes.

*

You go to the woods
you thought you knew
and someone else
is hiking there
shaking their bells.

And every geriatric
stereotype is true
except they aren't
from the inside, barring
your shoulder, your knee
a vertebra or two.

You knew the way
and now you're not sure
maybe not. It's all a little
foggy beyond caring.
Impressionistic will do.

But those nimble others
even kindly, look at you
funny, or not at all.

It is, after all, a world of din
din din din

No place for subtlety
complexity. Craftspersonship
was lost generations ago.

But the dancing young
are certain of their time— love, lust
hegemony, apocalyptic visions
important melancholy—
without any idea
it's a moment.

*

How soft should melancholy be?
Is *disappointment* even a word?
I'm not talking about mine
but yours and mine. Our cruelty
to each other is impeccable.
The animals lie splayed.
We've invaded and terrorized
plasticized, burned the feathers
off hope, arrogant and fat.
Melancholy is a belated whisper
at the edge of rage.
No words are heard
in the din.

NOTES

Insomnia, page 9
line 59, *to sleep: perchance to dream,* "Hamlet", Act III, Scene I, Wm Shakespeare.

Kicked Out By a Cloud, page 16
lines 15 & 16, *I watch the days/follow one another home like cowbells,* likely an allusion to *The cowbells follow one another/ Into the distances of the afternoon...* "Lying in a Hammock at William Duffy's Farm in Pine Island, Minnesota", James Wright, 1966.

In Concert – Mozart, page 21
Courtesy of Spuyten Duyvil Publishers, *An Æsthetic of Stone,* 2020
line 62, *Renascence, Recuerdo,* allusion to Edna St. Vincent Millay, 1912, 1920.

In Concert – Beethoven, page 33
line 9, *Howl, howl, howl...,* King Lear, Act V, Scene III, Wm Shakespeare.

Cat Quartet, page 46
line 18, Allusion to, *It takes a village to raise a child,* African proverb.

Bird News, page 49
line 60, *Perhaps it was just a sad day in Birdville,* allusion to, *But there is no joy in Mudville,* "Casey at the Bat", E.L. Thayer, 1888.

All Your Names, page 56
line 15, *...rosemary, that's for remembrance,* Hamlet, Act IV, Scene 5, Wm Shakespeare.
line 39, *What's in a name?,* Romeo and Juliet, Act II, Scene I,
Wm Shakespeare.
last line, *...where the mountain hare has lain,* "Memory", W.B. Yeats, 1917.

Perhaps one Writes, page 66

lines 4&5, see: en.wikipedia.org/wiki/If_a_tree_falls_in_a_forest

Poetry, page 67

lines 7 &17, *in times like these*, allusion to "What Kind of Times are These?", Adrienne Rich, 1995.

line 19*ff*, "Depressed by a Book of Bad Poetry, I Walk Toward an Unused Pasture and Invite the Insects to Join Me", James Wright, 1963.

Blurb, page 69

line 8 & 9, "All happy families are alike; each unhappy family is unhappy in its own way." Leo Tolstoy, *Anna Karenina,* 1877.

Process, page 70

Epigraph, *To do something very common, in my own way,* "A Valediction Forbidding Mourning", Adrienne Rich, 1970.

The Art of Being Satisfied With What You Have, page 75

Allusion to Kurt Vonnegut's Obituary/Poem for Joseph Heller, *The New Yorker,* May 16, 2005

Din, page 84

Section 3, 1st stanza, allusion to "Stopping by Woods on a Snow Evening", Robert Frost, 1923.

Section 4, line 11, allusion to "'Hope' is the Thing with Feathers", Emily Dickinson, 1891.

LAURI ROBERTSON has written poetry for many years–
Adrienne Rich was her mentor. Her first book, *An
Æsthetic of Stone,* was published by Spuyten Duyvil last
year. Two new pre-2020 volumes, *Where Do the Memories
Go?* and *In Concert,* are now offered in tandem. Lauri
is a psychiatrist/psychoanalyst formerly on the clinical
faculty of Yale Medical School. She's also a fine art
photographer, represented on Nantucket Island by The
Gallery at Four India: laurirobertsonphotography.com

www.ingramcontent.com/pod-product-compliance
Lightning Source LLC
Chambersburg PA
CBHW012101090526
44592CB00017B/2650